citrus essentials

Rio Nuevo Publishers®
P.O. Box 5250, Tucson, Arizona 85703-0250
(520) 623-9558, www.rionuevo.com

Text and photography © 2006 by Rio Nuevo Publishers. Food styling by Tracy
Vega. Many thanks to AJ's Fine Foods and to Jeannine Brookshire for providing
beautiful settings and amenities for the photo shoots for this book.

Photography credits as follows:
Mary Humphreys: page 4 (right), 38-39
W. Ross Humphreys: pages 2-3, 4 (left), 10, 12-13, 18-19, 21, 36, 50,
53, 54-55, 68-69, 77, back cover
Robin Stancliff: pages 5, 22, 25, 32, 35, 47, 59, front cover

Library of Congress Cataloging-in-Publication Data

Noble, Marilyn.
Citrus essentials / Marilyn Noble.
    p. cm. — (Cook west series)
Includes index.
ISBN-13: 978-1-887896-91-7 (pbk.)
ISBN-10: 1-887896-91-0 (pbk.)
1. Cookery (Citrus fruits) 2. Cookery, American—Southwestern
style.   I. Title. II. Series.
TX813.C5N62 2006
641.6'4304—dc22

                                                    2005037701

Design: Karen Schober, Seattle, Washington.
Printed in Korea.10 9 8 7 6 5 4 3 2 1

citrus
essentials

MARILYN NOBLE

RIO NUEVO PUBLISHERS
TUCSON, ARIZONA

COOK WEST
SERIES

contents

xxxxxx

Ah, citrus...one of nature's most sensual fruits. What's more heavenly than the intoxicating fragrance of an orange grove in full bloom? Or the sweet-spicy flavor of a luscious ruby-red grapefruit, pulled from the tree and peeled on the spot? Or the comforting perfection of a box of bright orange clementines sitting on the kitchen counter in the dead of winter, when everything outside is cold and gray?

My love affair with citrus started when I was a young girl, growing up in the desert Southwest. I would help my grandmother and my mother juice lemons for iced tea or for the delicious lemon meringue pie that was a summertime staple for dessert. One of my favorite pastimes was to carry a fat, juicy orange and a Nancy Drew book up into my favorite tree, where I would read for hours. And every Christmas morning there was the obligatory tangerine in the stocking, along with the candy cane and chocolate kisses. My sisters tended to ignore the fruit and go right for the candy, but I discovered that chocolate with tangerine was a match made in heaven.

When I was old enough to cook in my own kitchen, I learned that citrus went with almost anything, from canned tuna to the most elegant chocolate-orange cake. Even when I don't have much time for cooking elaborate meals, I add lemon, orange, or lime juice to a wide variety of salad dressings and marinades to liven up what we eat every day. A small amount of juice or grated peel can change the character of baked sweets or grilled meats.

Unlike many things that provide such a great eating experience, citrus is also healthy. One orange can provide more than the recommended daily allowance of vitamin C, along with generous doses of fiber, potassium, calcium, carotene, and folic acid. A tablespoon of lemon juice combined with two tablespoons of honey makes a soothing and natural cough syrup, and pure lemon juice applied to the face exfoliates, tightens pores, and fades freckles and age spots. It also adds vitamin C to the skin, which many experts claim reduces the signs of aging.

HISTORY

The earliest known written reference to citrus comes from Chinese emperor Ta Yu, who ruled around 2200 B.C. More than 3,000 years later, explorers carried citrus back to the Mediterranean, where it was prized for its medicinal purposes and became a sought-after trading item. Because citrus hybridizes easily, those early species soon evolved into the lemons, limes, oranges, grapefruit, tangerines, and other cultivars that we know today.

Spain and Italy became major citrus-producing regions, and when Columbus came to the New World, he brought along seeds, giving birth to a major food crop in the southern United States. Today, citrus is grown throughout the world—including commercially in parts of California, Arizona, and Texas—and is used not only for food, but also for essential oils used in perfumes, cleaning products, and insect repellents. Who hasn't burned citronella candles to chase away those annoying mosquitoes that mar an otherwise lovely evening on the patio?

TYPES OF CITRUS

While there are dozens of subspecies of citrus, many of them aren't used for food purposes, so I'll concentrate on the most common varieties, all widely available year-round in most grocery stores (even though citrus is considered a winter crop). Because many types of citrus can stay viable on the tree for so long, the harvest actually runs from October until as late as June for some varieties.

Sweet Orange This is the most widely grown citrus fruit in the world, and almost all of the oranges that we use for eating, juicing, or cooking fall into this category. Navels, Valencias, and blood oranges (named for their dark red flesh) are easy to find. When a recipe specifies fresh orange juice, look for Valencias or other seeded varieties, because they are generally juicier than seedless oranges such as navels, which are good for eating out of the hand.

Lemon Grown throughout the Mediterranean region and Mexico, lemons are another widely available and useful fruit. They keep well in the refrigerator, and it's always nice to have a couple on hand for adding zest to a recipe, squeezing into a glass of ice water on a hot day, or sprinkling over the bottom of a copper pan and then scrubbing with salt to take away the tarnish. Lemon has the highest concentration of vitamin C of any of the fruits in the citrus family, a fact not lost on the Royal Navy when sailing ships roamed the seas. Before ships left port, they were well stocked with lemons to prevent scurvy in the crew. At the time, lemons were thought to be under-ripe limes, hence the nickname for British sailors—"limeys."

Lime We have two commonly available types in this country: Persian and Key. Persian limes are bigger and thicker skinned, with less aromatic oil in the peel and comparatively less juice. Key limes, also known as Mexican limes, are preferred for these recipes because of their superior flavor and strength. It's also much easier to force a wedge of Mexican lime than Persian into a bottle of Corona.

Grapefruit This accidental hybrid with the unfortunate misnomer has become a popular and standard component of Southwestern cooking and eating. The pulp ranges in color from pale yellow to deep red, and the sweetness differs greatly between varieties. It's also a good keeper if refrigerated.

Mandarin Orange (Tangerine) Believed to be one of the original species of citrus, these sweet, juicy fruits originated in Asia, where many are still grown today. They don't keep as well as the others, so they may be only seasonally available in fresh form, but they're wonderful for snacking. In the U.S., the fresh fruits are commonly called tangerines, while the canned ones are called mandarin oranges. Clementines, satsumas, and dancy oranges are related cultivars. Because tangerines are usually small and seedy, and have a loose peel, they're not very practical for cooking purposes, but they make a great Christmas stocking stuffer. Just be sure to include the chocolate.

Sour Orange These are also known as Seville oranges, and you probably won't run across these at the grocery store often because the season is very short. They're primarily used for making marmalade, and the essential oils are used to flavor liqueurs like Grand Marnier and Triple Sec. Oil from one variety, Bergamot, is also used as the main flavoring in Earl Grey tea.

Tangelos A cross between the sweet orange and the grapefruit, these are also a short-season fruit. Like tangerines, they're not the best for cooking, but great for eating.

Look for fruit that feels heavy and has unblemished skin, with no shrinking or shriveling.

Bring to room temperature before juicing, to get more juice.

Rolling the fruit on the counter to break up the pulp will also help increase the juice yield.

Invest in a zester, a small tool that scrapes the peel from the fruit and leaves the bitter white membrane behind.

You can freeze both the juice and the zest for later use. To freeze the juice, pour into ice-cube trays. Once it's solid, place it in a freezer bag. One cube is about equal to one tablespoon. For zest, freeze in plastic bags and measure it out as you need it.

Since the acidic nature of the fruit causes it to "cook" meat and seafood, avoid marinating for longer than the recommended times.

To get sections, also known as "supremes," peel the fruit, removing all of the white membrane from the outside, and then run a sharp knife between the sections, loosening them from the membrane. Do this over a bowl to capture the excess juice. If the recipe doesn't call for juice, freeze it to use later.

If you're using a large number of oranges, lemons, limes, or grapefruit, and the recipe doesn't call for zest, then go ahead and zest the fruit anyway, and freeze it for later use.

Experiment and have fun! The tang of citrus makes a nice counterpoint to the heat of chiles and the smokiness of the grill, which is why it's such a versatile and necessary part of Southwestern cuisine.

TIPS FOR COOKING WITH CITRUS

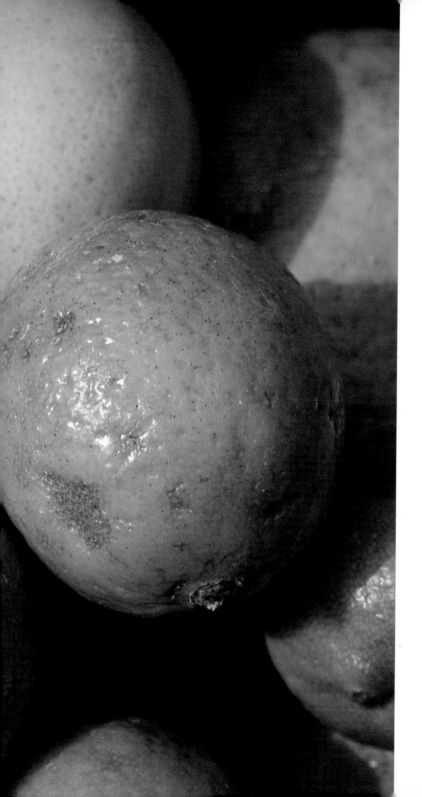

For Starters

xxxxxx

Ceviche

xxxxxx

Serves 6

½ pound fresh medium shrimp, peeled and deveined

½ pound fresh medium scallops

½ pound firm white fish, skinned and cut into 1-inch chunks

1 cup fresh lime juice

⅓ cup chopped red onion

2 tomatoes, finely chopped

2 fresh jalapeños, seeds and ribs removed, finely chopped

½ yellow pepper, finely chopped

1 avocado, finely chopped

½ cup extra-virgin olive oil

1 tablespoon minced cilantro

1 clove garlic, minced

½ teaspoon salt

¼ teaspoon freshly ground black pepper

1 teaspoon red pepper flakes

2 bay leaves

This reminds me of many happy hours on the beach in Mexico, sitting under a palapa with a cold Pacifico and a platter of fish "cooked" in lime juice. This presentation is a little more refined, but the spirit is still there. Use the freshest seafood you can find, and don't forget the cerveza!

Combine shrimp, scallops, and fish in a glass dish, then cover them with lime juice. Refrigerate for 8 hours.

Drain the seafood mixture and combine with the red onion, tomatoes, jalapeños, yellow pepper, and avocado.

Whisk together the olive oil, cilantro, garlic, salt, pepper, and red pepper flakes in a small bowl; add the bay leaves after whisking. Pour this over the fish mixture and refrigerate for 1 hour.

Drain the ceviche and remove the bay leaves.

For each serving, line a stemmed glass with lettuce leaves, then spoon in some ceviche. Garnish with a sprig of cilantro and a wedge of lime, and serve with a basket of hot tortilla chips.

Jicama with Limes

xxxxxx

Jicama is a root vegetable with a sweet taste and crunchy texture, available in most grocery stores. The smaller and heavier they are, the better they taste.

Peel and slice the jicama, then sprinkle it with lime juice. Sift together the chile powder, cayenne, and salt, then dust over the jicama. Garnish with lime wedges.

Serves 6

1 small jicama, peeled and julienned

Juice of 2 limes

1 tablespoon red chile powder

$1/2$ teaspoon cayenne pepper

$1/2$ teaspoon salt
1 lime, sliced into wedges, for garnish

Kitchen Sink Guacamole

xxxxxx

The wonderful thing about guacamole is that you can throw anything and everything into it, just like the kitchen sink.

Peel and pit the avocados and slice into a bowl, then squeeze lime juice over all. Mash with a fork to a smooth consistency. Add the onions, garlic, jalapeños, tomatoes, and olives. Add salt and pepper to taste, and mix well. Line a small serving platter with lettuce leaves and mound guacamole in the center. Surround with tortilla chips.

Serves 8

4 large ripe avocados

Juice of 1 lime

1 bunch green onions

1 clove garlic, mashed

2 fresh jalapeños, seeded and diced

2 tomatoes, peeled, seeded, and chopped

1 small can sliced black olives

Salt and pepper

Lettuce leaves, for garnish

Easy Guacamole

xxxxxx

Makes 1 cup

2 large avocados

Juice of 1/2 lemon

1 clove garlic, mashed

1 tablespoon
minced onion

Salt

If you want a quick snack or a filler for tacos or tostados, this is the perfect guacamole. It's also great with grilled meats or fish.

Peel and pit, then mash the avocados with a fork. Blend in the lemon juice, garlic, onion, and salt to taste. Serve immediately.

Mango Peach Salsa

xxxxxx

Makes 3 cups

1 ripe mango,
peeled
and diced

2 peaches, peeled
and diced

Juice of 2 limes

1 red bell pepper,
seeded and diced

1 or 2 fresh habañeros,
seeded and diced

1/2 cup cilantro, chopped

1 bunch green onions,
thinly sliced, tops included

This one has a bite to it, but the heat of the habañero is offset by the sweetness of the mango and peaches. If you want a less spicy salsa, substitute a jalapeño for the habañero. And don't forget that when you handle hot peppers, you should wear a pair of disposable gloves.

Combine the diced mango and peaches, then stir in the lime juice. Add the bell pepper, habañeros, cilantro, and onions. Serve with chips.

This also makes a nice condiment for fish tacos and grilled shrimp.

Shrimp Pâté

xxxxxx

The jalapeño gives just a hint of heat.

Serves 6

Using a food processor, combine all ingredients except the shrimp and process until smooth and fluffy. Remove from processor and stir in the shrimp. Chill before serving.

1 package cream cheese (4 ounces), softened

2 tablespoons lemon juice

$1/2$ teaspoon horseradish

1 green onion, thinly sliced

3 tablespoons mayonnaise

1 hard-boiled egg

$1/4$ teaspoon salt

1 fresh jalapeño, seeded and finely chopped

1 pound cooked shrimp, shelled, deveined, and chopped

Avocado Crab Dip

xxxxxx

This one is great served with whole-grain crackers.

Makes 2½ cups

Mash the avocado with the lemon juice, then stir in the onion and jalapeño. Add the Worcestershire sauce, cream cheese, and sour cream, blending well. Stir in the crabmeat.

1 large avocado, mashed

1 tablespoon fresh lemon juice

2 tablespoons minced green onion

1 fresh jalapeño, seeded and minced

1 teaspoon Worcestershire sauce

1 package cream cheese (8 ounces), softened

$1/2$ cup sour cream

1 can crabmeat ($7 1/2$ ounces), drained and flaked

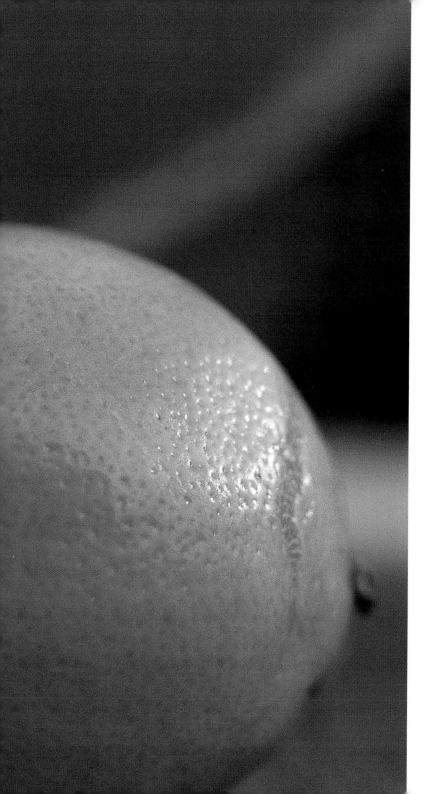

The Main Event

xxxxxx

Salmon Ensenada

xxxxxx

Serves 6

12 dry corn husks

1 cup dry white wine

Juice of 2 limes

1/4 cup extra-virgin olive oil

1/4 teaspoon salt

1 tablespoon dried dill, or 1 teaspoon fresh

6 salmon fillets

2 limes, sliced

The salmon fillets steam inside the corn husks, giving them a delightful, moist texture, but they still have a hint of grilled taste.

Soak the corn husks in cold water until moist and pliable, about 1 hour.

Whisk together the wine, lime juice, olive oil, salt, and dill, then pour this mixture over the salmon in a glass baking dish. Marinate for no more than 30 minutes, turning the fish once.

Heat the grill to medium-high. Drain the corn husks. For each serving, overlap 2 husks and place 1 salmon fillet in the middle. Cover the fish with lime slices, then wrap it in the husks and fasten with toothpicks.

Place each fillet on the grill, then cover. Turn once, cooking approximately 4 minutes on each side, depending on the thickness of the fillets.

Grilled Shrimp Kebabs

xxxxxx

Because the shrimp and vegetables cook differently, I like to put them on separate skewers. When they're done, I remove the skewers and put everything on a large, warmed serving platter.

Combine the olive oil, wine, lemon juice, garlic, onion, soy sauce, and hot pepper sauce for the marinade, then pour the mixture over the shrimp in a glass container. Marinate 2–3 hours.

Heat the grill to medium-hot. Drain the shrimp, reserving the marinade. Place the shrimp on skewers, then do the same for the mushrooms, bell peppers, onion, and tomatoes.

Place the skewers on the grill and baste frequently with the reserved marinade until the shrimp are pink and the vegetables are tender, approximately 6 minutes for the shrimp and 10 minutes for the vegetables.

Serves 4

$1/2$ cup extra-virgin olive oil

$1/2$ cup dry white wine

$1/4$ cup lemon juice

1 clove garlic, crushed

$1/4$ cup minced onion

$1/4$ cup soy sauce

Dash of hot pepper sauce

2 pounds jumbo shrimp, peeled and deveined

12 mushrooms

2 green bell peppers, each cut into 6 chunks

1 red onion, cut into 12 chunks

12 cherry tomatoes

Seared Sea Scallops with Jalapeño Lime Aioli

xxxxxx

Serves 4

A light and simple dinner served with crusty bread and a hearty salad.

2 tablespoons olive oil

20 large sea scallops

Salt and pepper

Jalapeño Lime Aioli
(see page 51)

Heat the olive oil in a large skillet until hot, then add the scallops. Sear on each side after sprinkling with salt and pepper to taste.

Squeeze Jalapeño Lime Aioli onto plates in an attractive pattern, then place the scallops on the plates and squeeze more aioli over the top.

Grilled Orange Turkey with Piñon Nut Stuffing

xxxxxx

Serves 6

1 fresh turkey
(12–14 pounds)

1 stick of butter,
softened

1 orange, cut into
eighths, peel on

1 apple, cored and sliced

1 onion, quartered

Salt

2 cups fresh orange juice

1 cup white wine

If you're lucky enough to live in a warm climate at Thanksgiving, grilling the turkey is a nice alternative to oven roasting. If it's too cold to fire up the grill, you can also do this in the oven; just follow the directions that come with the turkey. The Orange-Cranberry Relish (see page 48) and the Lime-Glazed Sweet Potatoes (see page 49) make perfect accompaniments. Serve with Piñon Nut Stuffing (recipe follows). You will want to make your cornbread for the stuffing the day before you plan to cook the turkey. If you're roasting the turkey in the oven, you can either stuff the turkey or bake the stuffing in a separate pan.

Using indirect heat method (with the lid closed and the meat positioned away from the fire), place a foil drip pan in the grill and preheat to medium.

Prepare the turkey by removing the giblets, rinsing, and patting dry. Work the softened butter underneath the turkey skin, then place the orange, apple, and onion pieces in the body cavity. Sprinkle with salt, tuck the wing ends under, and secure the legs.

Insert a meat thermometer into the breast or thigh, taking care not to touch bone, and making sure that it won't interfere with the grill cover. Place the turkey on the grill over the drip pan and cover the grill. Baste periodically with a mixture of the orange juice and white wine, and roast until the thermometer reads 170 degrees F, approximately 3–4 hours. Remove from the grill and allow to stand for about 30 minutes before carving.

PIÑON NUT STUFFING

One day in advance, prepare cornbread according to the directions on a box of cornmeal, omitting the sugar. Let it cool in the pan overnight.

To prepare the stuffing, crumble the cornbread into a large bowl, then shred the white bread and combine it with the cornbread. Set aside.

In a large skillet, melt the butter and sauté the onion, bell pepper, celery, and jalapeños until they are soft and fragrant, about 5 minutes. Add the vegetables to the bread mixture and stir to combine. Whisk the eggs together, then add them to bread mixture, stirring until well blended. Moisten with warm vegetable stock until the mixture is very wet. Stir in salt and sage, then add piñon nuts.

Bake in a buttered baking dish at 350 degrees F for 1 hour.

Serves 8–10

1 pan of cornbread
(9 x 9 inches)

1 loaf white bread

1 stick butter

1 medium onion, minced

1 bell pepper, diced

3 celery ribs, sliced

3 fresh jalapeños, seeded
and minced

3 eggs

1/2 cup vegetable stock

1 teaspoon salt

1 tablespoon rubbed sage

1 cup piñon nuts

Chicken El Charro

xxxxxx

Serves 6

½ cup fresh lime juice

½ cup tequila

2 tablespoons extra-virgin olive oil

½ teaspoon salt

¼ teaspoon pepper

1 clove garlic, crushed

6 boneless, skinless chicken breasts

Be careful not to over-marinate—the chicken will turn mushy. If you have any leftovers, slice them up and use for salad the next day.

Whisk together the lime juice, tequila, olive oil, salt, pepper, and garlic. Pour this mixture over the chicken breasts in a glass dish. Cover and refrigerate 30 minutes, turning the chicken several times.

Heat the grill to medium-high. Remove the chicken from the marinade, reserving the liquid. Cook chicken for about 8 minutes, turning frequently and basting with the reserved marinade until done.

Lemon Chicken Topopo

xxxxxx

This is a slightly different twist on the traditional topopo salad that you'll find on the menus at most Mexican restaurants in Arizona.

Place the chicken breasts in a deep skillet and cover with the water. Add the lemon juice, salt, pepper, and red pepper flakes. Cover and bring to a simmer, poaching gently until the chicken is cooked, about 25 minutes. Cool, then slice across the grain into strips. (This can be prepared 1 day ahead.)

Heat the oil in a deep skillet, and then fry the tortillas, one at a time, until crisp. Drain them well on paper towels.

To assemble the salads, place a tortilla in the middle of each of 4 plates, then top each one with black beans. Add a mound of lettuce, then arrange the sliced chicken, avocado, tomato wedges, black olives, green onions, and *queso fresco* on top of each. Drizzle with Lemon Vinaigrette Dressing.

Serves 4

4 boneless, skinless chicken breasts

2 cups water

Juice of 1 lemon

1/2 teaspoon salt

1/4 teaspoon white pepper

1 teaspoon red pepper flakes

1/2 cup vegetable oil

4 corn tortillas

1 can black beans, drained and rinsed

8 cups shredded romaine lettuce

2 avocados, peeled, seeded, and sliced lengthwise

2 large tomatoes, cut into wedges

2 small cans sliced black olives

1 bunch green onions

1 cup crumbled *queso fresco* or feta cheese

Lemon Vinaigrette Dressing (see page 51)

Lemon Risotto

xxxxxx

Serves 6

1 medium onion, minced

1 stick butter

5 cups chicken broth

2 cups Arborio rice

1 cup white wine

1 lemon, juiced and zested

1 teaspoon salt

1 cup grated Asiago cheese

Risotto comes from the Veneto region of Italy, but the lemon in this version gives it a sunny flavor that reminds me of sitting on the patio at a winery, sipping a wonderful Sauvignon Blanc. For the best result, avoid buying the grated, packaged Asiago and spring for a nice chunk that you grate yourself. Risotto is easy, if somewhat labor-intensive, but it's well worth it.

In a large skillet, sauté the onion in butter until soft and translucent. While the onion is cooking, place the chicken broth in a large saucepan and heat to a slow simmer.

Add the rice to the onion and butter and stir for 1 minute, until the rice is coated. Keep the heat low enough that the rice doesn't begin to brown. Add the wine, lemon juice, and grated lemon zest. Continue stirring until the wine is absorbed and the rice is beginning to look dry. Ladle ½ cup of broth into the rice, and continue to stir, taking care to scrape the bottom and sides of the pan so the rice doesn't stick. When liquid is absorbed and the rice looks dry, add another ladle of stock. Continue the process of ladling and stirring for about 20 minutes.

Taste a grain of rice. It should be tender with no crunch. If it's still not done, continue adding stock and stirring. If you run out of stock, use hot water.

Once the rice has reached a creamy consistency and is tender, season with salt and add the cheese. Stir until the cheese is blended, remove from heat, and serve immediately in warm bowls.

Carbonada Criolla

xxxxxx

You'll find as many versions of this traditional Argentine meat stew as there are cooks. Almost every version includes sweet potatoes and some form of fruit. Ours has oranges, which give the dish a Southwestern zing.

Heat the oil in a Dutch oven and brown the meat in batches, draining well after cooking. Set aside. Add the onion, garlic, bell pepper, and tomatoes to the same pan and cook until soft. Add the stock, wine, cilantro, oregano, crushed red chiles, salt, and pepper, then bring to a boil, stirring and scraping the bottom of the pan. When the mixture reaches a full boil, add the browned pork, reduce heat to simmer, cover, and cook for 30 minutes, stirring occasionally. Add the sweet potatoes and simmer for another 15 minutes, covered, then add the zucchini, yellow squash, corn, peaches, and oranges. Cook for another 10 minutes, until the squash is tender.

Serve with a salad and lots of crusty whole-grain bread.

Serves 8

2 tablespoons
extra-virgin olive oil

3 pounds boneless pork
loin, cut into 1-inch cubes

1 medium onion, diced

6 cloves garlic, minced

1 medium green bell
pepper, seeded and chopped

4 tomatoes, chopped

3 cups chicken stock

1 cup white wine

1 teaspoon minced cilantro

1 teaspoon oregano

$1/2$ teaspoon
crushed dried red chiles

1 teaspoon salt

$1/4$ teaspoon pepper

3 sweet potatoes, peeled
and cut into 1-inch chunks

1 zucchini, sliced into
$1/2$-inch pieces

1 yellow squash, sliced
into $1/2$-inch pieces

2 ears of corn, cut into
1-inch pieces

2 large peaches,
peeled and diced

2 seedless oranges,
sliced with the peel on

Orange Grilled Pork Chops

xxxxxx

The smoky heat of the chipotles is nicely balanced by the sweetness of orange and the tanginess of lime.

Make marinade by combining the orange juice, chipotles, brown sugar, and lime juice in a food processor. Blend until smooth. Pour the marinade over the pork chops in a glass dish and allow to marinate for 1 hour, turning once. Drain and reserve the marinade.

Heat the grill to medium-high and grill the chops, basting frequently and taking care not to let the sugar in the marinade burn. Total grilling time should be about 9 minutes for 1-inch-thick chops.

Serves 6

1 cup fresh orange juice

2 canned chipotles in adobo sauce

3 tablespoons brown sugar

1 tablespoon fresh lime juice

6 center-cut pork loin chops, boneless

Carne Asada Tacos with Pico de Gallo

xxxxxx

Serves 4

2 pounds top sirloin,
sliced thin

Juice of 6 limes

1 teaspoon garlic powder

2 tablespoons olive oil

8 small flour tortillas or
gorditas

1 can black beans, drained,
rinsed, and warmed

Pico de Gallo (recipe follows)

Easy Guacamole
(see page 16)

Most Mexican cooks use skirt steak for carne asada, but top sirloin is generally easier to find and to handle. You can adjust the heat of the Pico de Gallo by increasing or decreasing the number of jalapeños. The pomegranate adds a touch of color and sweetness.

Sprinkle the steaks with the lime juice and garlic powder, then let them sit at room temperature for 30 minutes. Heat the oil in a large skillet over high heat, then sear the sirloin slices about 30 seconds on each side until done.

Warm the flour tortillas and beans. Serve with plenty of Pico de Gallo and guacamole for do-it-yourself tacos.

PICO DE GALLO

Makes 2 cups

4 large tomatoes,
peeled and chopped

1/2 cup minced sweet onion

1 clove garlic, minced

4 pickled
jalapeños, chopped

1/4 cup minced cilantro

1/4 cup pomegranate
seeds (optional)

Salt to taste

Combine all ingredients and refrigerate for several hours to allow the flavors to blend.

California Flank Steak

xxxxxx

Serve this with warm flour tortillas or crusty individual French rolls. You could even layer it on a bed of greens for a tasty steak salad.

Place steak in a non-reactive dish. Whisk together the lime juice, olive oil, garlic, cilantro, pepper, salt, and chile powder, and pour this mixture over the steak. Allow to marinate for 2 hours, turning the steak several times.

Heat grill to medium-high. Drain the marinade and place the steak on the grill for about 5 minutes for medium, turning once. Thinly slice across the grain to serve.

Serves 6

3 pounds flank steak

1 cup fresh lime juice

1/4 cup olive oil

1 clove garlic, crushed

1/2 cup chopped cilantro

1/4 teaspoon black pepper

1/2 teaspoon salt

1 tablespoon chile powder

On the Side
xxxxxx

Raspberry Orange Salad

xxxxxx

Serves 6 *A great salad for summertime dinner on the patio.*

8 cups mixed salad greens

1/2 red onion, thinly sliced

1 orange, peeled, sectioned into supremes, and sliced into 1/2-inch pieces

1 cup fresh raspberries

3/4 cup piñon nuts

3 tablespoons balsamic vinegar

1/2 cup olive oil

1/8 teaspoon dry mustard

1/2 teaspoon red chile powder

1 tablespoon orange juice

6 fresh raspberries

Assemble the salad by combining the greens, onion, orange pieces, 1 cup of raspberries, and piñon nuts.

To make dressing, combine the vinegar, oil, mustard, chile powder, orange juice, and the remaining 6 raspberries in a small screw-top jar; shake the mixture until the raspberries are broken up and the dressing is well blended. Pour over the salad and toss, taking care not to overdress. The salad should be moist, but not wet.

Sunshine Slaw

xxxxxx

This fresh-tasting alternative to the usual coleslaw makes a nice accompaniment to anything grilled. Because it has no mayonnaise, it's also a wonderful picnic dish.

Assemble the dressing by whisking together the juices, orange zest, and olive oil until well blended. Toss with the cabbage, sprinkle with salt and pepper to taste, then add the dates and pecans. Refrigerate for 30 minutes to allow the flavors to blend.

Serves 8

1/4 cup fresh orange juice

1 tablespoon fresh lime juice

1 tablespoon grated orange zest

3 tablespoons extra-virgin olive oil

5 cups finely shredded red cabbage

Salt and pepper

1/2 cup pitted and minced dates

1/2 cup chopped pecans

Jicama Orange Salad

xxxxxx

Serves 6

2 large oranges

1 red bell pepper,
sliced into rings

1 yellow bell pepper,
sliced into rings

1 orange bell pepper,
sliced into rings

1 small jicama,
peeled and julienned

2 tablespoons orange juice

1/2 cup extra-virgin olive oil

3 tablespoons
balsamic vinegar

2 teaspoons chile powder

1/4 teaspoon black pepper

Kalamata olives,
for garnish

A colorful, sweet, and crunchy accompaniment to anything grilled. Some of the juice you need for the dressing comes from the oranges when you slice them.

Peel the oranges and remove their outer membranes, then slice them, catching the juice. (Set the juice aside for the dressing.) Arrange the slices on a serving platter. Layer the bell pepper rings over the top, and finish with jicama matchsticks.

Whisk together the orange juice, olive oil, vinegar, chile powder, and pepper until blended, then pour over the assembled salad. Garnish with Kalamata olives.

Festive Fruit Salad

xxxxxx

This is great for brunch or lunch to accompany eggs Benedict or a hearty omelette.

Serves 6

Using a melon baller, scoop out the cantaloupe and honeydew. Rinse and hull the strawberries, and rinse the blackberries. Place the fruit in a deep bowl.

Combine the orange juice, orange and lemon zests, honey, and Grand Marnier, and pour the mixture over the fruit. Refrigerate for 3–4 hours, stirring occasionally.

1 ripe cantaloupe

1 ripe honeydew

1 pint fresh strawberries

1 pint fresh blackberries

$1/2$ cup fresh orange juice

$1/2$ teaspoon grated orange zest

$1/2$ teaspoon grated lemon zest

$1/4$ cup honey

1 teaspoon Grand Marnier

Spinach Salad Supreme

xxxxxx

Serves 6

This hearty salad can make a meal all by itself.

8 loosely packed cups
baby spinach leaves

6 hard-boiled eggs, diced

3 slices bacon, cooked
to crisp and crumbled

1 cup thinly
sliced mushrooms

1/2 cup sliced
Kalamata olives

2 large tomatoes,
cut into wedges

1/2 small red onion,
thinly sliced

1 clove garlic, crushed

2 tablespoons
minced cilantro

1 tablespoon lemon juice

3 tablespoons
white wine vinegar

1/2 cup extra-virgin olive oil

1/2 teaspoon salt

1/2 teaspoon chile powder

1/2 cup crumbled *queso
fresco* or feta cheese

Assemble the salad using the spinach, eggs, bacon, mushrooms, olives, tomatoes, and onion.

For the dressing, whisk together the garlic, cilantro, lemon juice, vinegar, oil, salt, and chile powder until well blended. Pour over the salad and toss, then top with the cheese.

Shrimp-Stuffed Avocados

xxxxxx

A lovely first course for dinner, this can also make a nice light lunch, served with sliced tomatoes that are drizzled with a little olive oil.

Cut the avocados in half and remove the pits, leaving the peels on. Slice the lemon in half and squeeze the juice of 1 half over the avocados. Cut the remaining half into 4 wedges to use as a garnish.

Blend together the sour cream, lemon juice, sugar, salt, and pepper. Add this dressing to the shrimp in small amounts, tossing to coat and moisten. Extra dressing can be stored in the refrigerator and used on green salad.

Mound the shrimp into the middle of each avocado half. Garnish with lemon wedges.

Serves 4

2 large, ripe avocados

1 lemon

1 cup sour cream

2 tablespoons fresh lemon juice

2 teaspoons sugar

$1/2$ teaspoon salt

$1/4$ teaspoon freshly ground black pepper

1 pound cocktail shrimp, cooked, peeled, and deveined

Avocado Grapefruit Salad

xxxxxx

Serves 4

2 avocados

2 ruby red grapefruit

1 tablespoon lemon juice

1 tablespoon white
wine vinegar

1/4 cup extra-virgin olive oil

1/2 teaspoon white pepper

Dash of brandy

Salt

12 cooked medium shrimp,
peeled and deveined

Toasted pecans, chopped

Red grapefruit is generally sweeter than its paler cousins. Look for heavy fruit with a pungent scent and unblemished peel.

Peel the avocados and slice them lengthwise. Peel the grapefruit, making sure to remove the white pith, and slice into 1/4-inch-thick slices.

Whisk together the lemon juice, vinegar, olive oil, and pepper. Add a dash of brandy and a pinch of salt to taste.

Arrange the avocado slices, grapefruit slices, and shrimp on chilled serving plates. Drizzle with dressing and top with toasted, chopped pecans.

Orange-Cranberry Relish

xxxxxx

Makes 4 cups

The bourbon adds a little kick to this traditional favorite.

1 bag of fresh cranberries (12 ounces)

1 cup sugar

1 cup fresh orange juice

Grated zest of 1 orange

2 tablespoons bourbon

Combine the cranberries, sugar, orange juice, and zest in a saucepan. Stir until blended, then cook over medium-high heat, stirring occasionally to prevent boiling over, until the cranberries burst and the sugar is dissolved, about 5 minutes. Remove from heat, cool, and add bourbon. Refrigerate until serving time.

Lime-Glazed Sweet Potatoes

xxxxxx

Many people think of sweet potatoes only at Thanksgiving, but with their abundance of nutrients, they make a healthy alternative to white potatoes.

Preheat the oven to 350 degrees F. Place the sweet potatoes in a large roasting pan and sprinkle with the juice of 1 lime, and salt and pepper to taste. Bake for about 15 minutes.

Meanwhile, heat the butter, ½ cup of lime juice, and brown sugar in a small saucepan. Cook until the sugar is dissolved and the mixture is slightly reduced. Remove from heat, then stir in the rum.

Pour the glaze over the sweet potatoes and return the dish to the oven, baking another 10–15 minutes until fork tender.

Serves 6

5 or 6 large sweet potatoes, scrubbed, peeled, and cut into chunks

Juice of 1 lime

Salt and pepper

2 tablespoons butter

$^1/_2$ cup fresh lime juice

$^1/_2$ cup brown sugar

$^1/_4$ cup dark rum

Jalapeño Lime Aioli

xxxxxx

You can use this on everything from hamburgers to fish tacos and grilled shrimp. It even adds a wonderful zip to an otherwise humdrum turkey sandwich.

Stir together all ingredients until well blended. Stored in a tightly covered container in the refrigerator, this keeps for about 2 weeks.

Makes 1 cup

1/2 cup sour cream

1/2 cup mayonnaise

Juice of 1 lime

1 clove garlic, crushed

1 fresh jalapeño, seeded and finely chopped

Lemon Vinaigrette Dressing

xxxxxx

Excellent for the Lemon Chicken Topopo salad on page 29, but also good drizzled over sliced avocado and red onion.

Whisk ingredients together in a small bowl. Serve immediately.

Makes 1 cup

1/2 cup extra-virgin olive oil

3 tablespoons white wine vinegar

1 tablespoon fresh lemon juice

1 clove garlic, crushed

1 small fresh jalapeño, seeded and finely chopped

1 tablespoon fresh parsley, finely minced

1/4 teaspoon salt

Pink Grapefruit Dressing

xxxxxx

Makes ½ cup

2 tablespoons sugar

3 shallots, minced

2 tablespoons honey

½ cup fresh pink grapefruit juice

¼ cup extra-virgin olive oil

2 tablespoons white wine vinegar

Juice of 1 lime

The sweet and sour flavor dresses up a simple plate of field greens and fresh fruit such as raspberries.

Melt the sugar in a small skillet, then add the shallots and honey. Cook for 1 minute, then add the grapefruit juice. Cook until reduced to a syrup. Remove from heat. Cool.

Puree in a food processor, and then, with the blade running, pour in the olive oil, vinegar, and lime juice.

Honey Mustard Grapefruit Dressing

xxxxxx

Makes 1 cup

2 tablespoons Dijon mustard

2 tablespoons warm honey

2 tablespoons fresh grapefruit juice

1 teaspoon chile powder

½ cup olive oil

Pinch of salt

A nice alternative to the traditional honey-mustard dressing you usually find adorning spinach salad.

Place all ingredients in a screw-top jar and shake until well blended. Serve immediately.

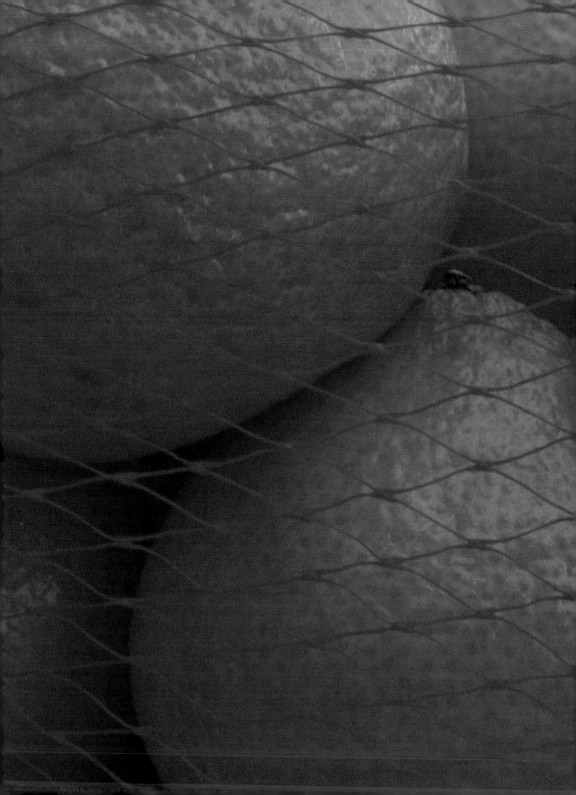

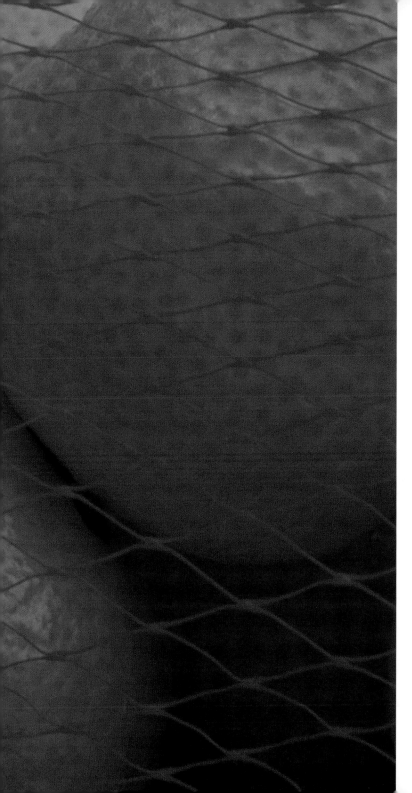

Sweet Things

xxxxxx

Lemon Berry Muffins

xxxxxx

Makes 12

½ cup chopped pecans

½ cup firmly packed brown sugar

¼ cup flour

2 teaspoons grated lemon zest

2 tablespoons butter, melted

1½ cups flour

½ cup firmly packed brown sugar

¼ cup sugar

1 teaspoon ground cinnamon

2 teaspoons baking powder

¼ teaspoon salt

2 teaspoons grated lemon zest

½ cup milk

1 stick of butter, melted and cooled

1 egg

1½ cups fresh raspberries, blueberries, and blackberries, in any combination

I make these every year for Mother's Day brunch. The kids love them, and so do the moms. I also get up early and bake them whenever we have house guests. It's a nice way to say "good morning."

Preheat the oven to 350 degrees F.

Toast the pecans in a hot skillet until lightly browned and fragrant.

In a small bowl, combine ½ cup of brown sugar, ¼ cup of flour, and 2 teaspoons of lemon zest for the topping, then stir in the toasted pecans and 2 tablespoons of melted butter. Set aside.

To make the batter, combine 1½ cups of flour, additional ½ cup of brown sugar, ¼ cup of sugar, cinnamon, baking powder, salt, and additional 2 teaspoons of lemon zest until well blended. Make a well in the center and add the milk, the melted stick of butter, and egg, mixing by hand until smooth. Carefully fold in the berries.

Spoon the thick batter into lined muffin tins, filling each about two-thirds full, then sprinkle with the topping mixture.

Bake for 25 minutes, until a toothpick inserted in the center of a muffin comes out clean.

Cool in the tins for 5 minutes, then remove and serve warm.

Glazed Grapefuit

xxxxxx

Although any honey will do, mesquite honey has a distinctive flavor that always reminds me of the desert after a rain.

Cut the grapefruits in half. Loosen sections by running a sharp knife between the flesh and each membrane. Place the grapefruit halves in a baking dish, then coat the top of each half with honey. Sprinkle with brown sugar and broil until the fruit begins to brown. Remove from the broiler and sprinkle each half with ginger.

Serves 4

2 large pink grapefruits

$1/4$ cup honey, preferably mesquite

2 tablespoons brown sugar

2 teaspoons minced crystallized ginger

French Toast with Grapefruit Syrup

xxxxxx

Serves 4 *Perfect for a lazy Sunday morning or breakfast at the pool.*

3 eggs

1/2 cup sugar

1/2 teaspoon vanilla extract

1 teaspoon ground cinnamon

2 cups half-and-half

8 thick slices day-old French bread

Butter for griddle

1 pink grapefruit

1/2 cup honey

1/2 cup cream cheese, softened

Whisk together the eggs, sugar, vanilla, cinnamon, and half-and-half. Place the bread slices in a large baking pan, then pour the egg batter over them. Turn once so that pieces are evenly coated, and allow to stand for a few minutes until the liquid is absorbed.

Heat a large griddle or skillet and coat with butter. Fry the bread pieces until brown on each side. Cover and keep warm.

Peel and section the grapefruit, removing the membranes. Place the sections in a saucepan with the honey, and heat until the honey is melted.

Cover each piece of toast with a layer of cream cheese, then top with the prepared grapefruit syrup.

Orange Berry Crepes

xxxxxx

Serves 6

1 cup flour

$^1/_2$ cup water

$^3/_4$ cup milk

2 large eggs

3 tablespoons unsalted butter, melted and cooled

2 tablespoons Triple Sec

2 tablespoons melted butter for cooking crepes

8 egg yolks

$^1/_4$ cup sugar

$^3/_4$ cup fresh orange juice

$^1/_4$ cup Triple Sec

2 cups fresh, seasonal berries, rinsed and well drained

Powdered sugar

This beautiful presentation is appropriate for a Champagne brunch or after-dinner dessert. Make the crepes a day or so in advance, and the rest is easy. Save the egg whites for a healthy omelette.

To make the crepes, combine the flour, water, milk, eggs, unsalted butter, and 2 tablespoons of Triple Sec in the bowl of a food processor, then pulse until well blended, about 20 seconds. Scrape down the sides and allow the batter to rest for an hour.

Brush an 8-inch skillet or crepe pan with some of the melted butter, then heat over medium-high until the pan begins to smoke. Pour ¼ cup of the batter into the hot pan, swirling to coat the bottom. Heat for about 45 seconds until the bottom is browned, then flip and cook the other side until lightly browned, about another 10 seconds. Remove from the pan and allow to cool on a flat surface. Continue cooking the remaining batter in the same fashion, brushing the pan with butter between each crepe.

Crepes can be stored in a stack separated by wax paper, then wrapped in plastic and placed in the refrigerator. They can also be frozen.

To make orange zabaglione filling for the crepes, combine the 8 egg yolks and the sugar in a round-bottom zabaglione pan, or in the top of a double boiler. Whisk until light yellow. Add the orange juice and ¼ cup of Triple Sec, and place the pan over simmering water, making sure the water doesn't touch the bottom of the pan. Continue to whisk briskly until the mixture doubles in volume and becomes thick enough to coat the bottom of a metal spoon, approximately 5 minutes. Whisk and cook another 3 minutes. Remove from heat and set aside to cool slightly.

Assemble the crepes by placing some berries down the middle of each, then folding the ends over to form a sort of "envelope" to enclose the berries. Pour ¼ cup of the warm zabaglione on each dessert plate, then place 3 crepes, seam side down, on top. Dust with powdered sugar, drizzle a little of the zabaglione over the top, and garnish with more berries.

Helado de Toronja (Grapefruit Ice Cream)

xxxxxx

Serves 6

Zest of 2 lemons

1 1/4 cups sugar

1 1/2 cups water

1 envelope
unflavored gelatin

1/3 cup cold water

3/4 cup fresh
grapefruit juice

1 1/2 cups heavy cream

Fresh mint leaves,
for garnish

One of my favorite Mexican foods is the ice cream you buy from the street vendors. This reminds me of that rich, sweet treat, with a little extra tang from the grapefruit.

Process the lemon zest and sugar in a food processor until minced. Combine this mixture with the 1½ cups of water, bring to a boil, and cook 3–4 minutes. Remove from heat.

Meanwhile, soften the gelatin in the cold water. Add this to the sugar syrup, stirring until dissolved, and then stir in the grapefruit juice. Allow to cool.

Finally, stir in the heavy cream and freeze according to your ice cream maker instructions.

As an alternative to using an ice cream maker, freeze the mixture in a shallow baking pan until hard, about 8 hours. Just before serving, process in a food processor until the consistency is mushy and soft. Garnish each serving with a sprig of mint and serve immediately.

Mexican Lemon Pie

xxxxxx

This is a traditional lemon meringue pie, but the added lemon zest in the crust gives it another dimension.

To make the pie shell, sift the flour, 1 tablespoon of sugar, and ½ teaspoon of salt into a food processor. With the blade running, add the butter, 1 piece at a time. Process until the mixture resembles coarse crumbs. Add 1 tablespoon of lemon zest and the lemon extract; then, with the blade still running, add ice water, 1 tablespoon at a time, until the mixture forms a large ball.

Remove the dough from the work bowl and shape it into a smooth ball, working in a little flour if it seems sticky. Wrap in plastic, then refrigerate for at least 1 hour or up to 2 days. Can also be frozen for up to 1 month.

Preheat the oven to 350 degrees F. Remove the dough from the refrigerator and allow it to stand for a few minutes at room temperature (allow more time if the dough is frozen). Roll out on a flour-covered pastry board to a 14-inch circle about ⅛-inch thick. Place in a chilled 9-inch pie pan, trim and crimp the edge, and pierce with a fork in several places. Cover the inside of the crust with foil and fill with pie weights or dry beans, taking care not to cover the edge of the crust with the foil. Bake until it is just beginning to brown, about 25–30 minutes. Remove the weights or beans and bake until golden brown, approximately 10 more minutes. Remove from the oven and cool completely.

To make the filling, whisk the egg yolks in a medium-size mixing bowl and set aside.

Makes 1 pie

1½ cups plus 2 tablespoons bleached all-purpose flour

1 tablespoon sugar

½ teaspoon salt

6 tablespoons unsalted butter, cut into ¼-inch pieces and chilled

1 tablespoon finely grated lemon zest

½ teaspoon lemon extract

5 tablespoons ice water, or as needed

4 egg yolks (reserve whites for meringue)

⅓ cup cornstarch

1½ cups water

1⅓ cups sugar

¼ teaspoon salt

3 tablespoons butter

½ cup lemon juice

1 tablespoon finely grated lemon zest

4 egg whites

¼ teaspoon cream of tartar

¼ cup sugar

1 teaspoon finely grated lemon zest

In a medium saucepan, whisk together the cornstarch, 1½ cups of water, 1⅓ cups of sugar, and ¼ teaspoon of salt. Over medium-high heat, bring the mixture to a boil, stirring frequently. Boil for 1 minute. Remove from heat and slowly add half of the hot mixture to the egg yolks, stirring constantly.

Return the new egg mixture to the saucepan with the remainder of the hot mixture and cook over low heat, stirring constantly, for 1 more minute. Remove from heat and gently stir in the 3 tablespoons of butter, the lemon juice, and the second tablespoon of zest until well combined. Pour mixture into the cooled pie shell.

Make meringue: Preheat the oven to 375 degrees F. Beat the egg whites until foamy, then add cream of tartar. Add ¼ cup of sugar, a little at a time, while beating until stiff peaks form. Cover the pie with meringue, making soft peaks and completely covering the filling. Sprinkle with the remaining teaspoon of lemon zest. Bake for 10–12 minutes or until the meringue is golden. Remove from the oven and cool on a wire rack. Make sure the pie is cooled completely before slicing.

Chocolate Elegance

xxxxxx

*In Mexican cooking, it's common to add cinnamon to choco-
late. This luscious dessert combines three of my favorite flavors: orange, chocolate, and cinnamon. You might be tempted
to check the oven while the cake is baking, but don't, because
it will fall. Set the timer, and when it goes off you can open the
oven and make sure the cake is done.*

Add the orange zest to the buttermilk, then let stand at room
temperature until called for later in the recipe.

Separate the eggs.

Preheat the oven to 350 degrees F. Line an 11 x 17 x 1-inch jelly-
roll pan with parchment.

Cream together the butter and the sugars at medium speed on
the mixer until the mixture is light and fluffy. Add the egg
yolks one at a time, beating well after each addition. Beat in
the vanilla.

Sift together the flour, baking soda, and salt, then add this to
the batter, alternating with the orange-infused buttermilk.

In a separate bowl, beat the egg whites until stiff peaks form.
Beat one-fourth of the egg whites into the batter, then gently
fold in the rest. Spread the batter in the prepared pan, sprinkle
with cinnamon, and bake until the top is lightly browned and
springs back when touched, approximately 25–30 minutes.
Remove from the oven and cool on a rack for 15 minutes.

Serves 8

Grated zest of 1 orange

1 cup buttermilk

3 eggs

1³/₄ sticks unsalted
butter, softened

1 cup granulated sugar

1 cup powdered sugar

1 teaspoon vanilla extract

2 cups all-purpose flour

1 teaspoon baking soda

¹/₂ teaspoon salt

2 teaspoons ground
cinnamon

1¹/₂ cups heavy cream

1 pound bittersweet
chocolate

Remove from the pan to another rack, and gently peel away the parchment. Cool completely.

To make ganache (for frosting), heat the heavy cream in a saucepan until barely simmering. While the cream heats, break the chocolate into pieces, place them in the food processor, and process until finely grated. With the processor running, pour the hot cream into the grated chocolate, and process until smooth and spreadable.

To assemble, cut the cooled cake in half and place one half on a serving plate, cinnamon side up. Cover with a thick layer of ganache. Place the remaining half on top of the ganache, also cinnamon side up, and cover the top and sides with the remaining ganache. Refrigerate until the chocolate is firm, then slice into servings.

Tangerine Dream

xxxxxx

This is my other favorite combination: tangerine and chocolate.   *Serves 6*

Combine the zest, sugar, and water in a saucepan and boil for 20 minutes. Stir in the tangerine and lemon juices. Remove from heat and allow to cool to room temperature. Stir in the 2 cups of heavy cream. Freeze in an ice cream maker according to the manufacturer's instructions. Alternatively, freeze the mixture in a shallow baking pan until firm, about 6 hours. Transfer it to a food processor and pulse until mixture is smooth. Refreeze for 4 hours, preparing the chocolate sauce before the 4 hours have elapsed (directions follow), then process again to a smooth consistency. Serve immediately with chocolate sauce and toasted almonds.

To make the chocolate sauce, bring the remaining cup of heavy cream to a simmer. Place the broken chocolate pieces in a food processor and grate them. With the blade running, pour in the cream and process until the sauce is smooth. Cool to room temperature before serving, or refrigerate. Warm slightly to pouring consistency, if necessary.

3 tablespoons grated tangerine zest

1 1/2 cups sugar

1 cup water

3 cups fresh tangerine juice

1/4 cup lemon juice

2 cups heavy cream

1 cup heavy cream

8 ounces dark chocolate, broken in pieces

Slivered, toasted almonds, for garnish

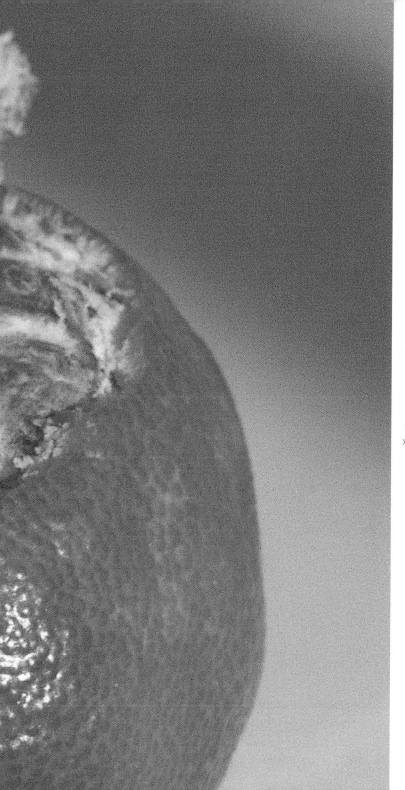

Thirst Quenchers

xxxxxx

Prickly Pear Lemonade

xxxxxx

Serves 6

3 cups fresh lemon juice

4 cups water

1 cup superfine sugar

$^1/_4$–$^1/_2$ cup prickly pear syrup

Lemon wedges and sugar for glass rims

Chilled club soda

Mint leaves, for garnish

Prickly pear syrup comes from the fruit of the prickly pear cactus. If you're lucky enough to live in the desert, you can harvest the fruit and make it yourself. If not, you can find it at some specialty food stores or order it online.

Combine the lemon juice, water, cup of sugar, and prickly pear syrup in a large pitcher. Rub the rim of each glass with a lemon wedge, then roll in sugar to coat. Add ice cubes to each glass, fill about ¾ full with lemonade mixture, then top off with club soda. Garnish each serving with a lemon wedge and mint leaves.

Farmhouse Iced Tea

xxxxxx

Serves 8

1 quart water

12 orange pekoe tea bags

1 cup fresh lemon juice

1 quart warm water

1 cup superfine sugar

2 lemons

Crushed ice

For every family gathering at my grandparents' house, my grandmother would make her farmhouse version of an Arnold Palmer. And I doubt that she even knew who he was.

Heat the first quart of water in a large saucepan. As the water heats, add the tea bags. When the water comes to a boil, remove from heat and allow to steep for 5 minutes, then remove the tea bags. The tea will be very strong.

Pour the tea into a large glass jar or pitcher. Add the lemon juice, remaining quart of water, and the sugar. Stir to dissolve. Slice the lemons and add them to the tea, then add crushed ice. Fill tall glasses with more ice, and pour in the tea.

The amount of sugar can be adjusted depending on taste.

Citrus Cooler

xxxxxx

A refreshing, non-alcoholic lunch or brunch drink.

Serves 8

Blend together the orange, grapefruit, and lime juices, add the sugar, and stir until dissolved. Add club soda, then pour over ice into tall glasses.

4 cups fresh orange juice

4 cups fresh grapefruit juice (pink or ruby red)

1 cup fresh lime juice

1 cup superfine sugar

1 quart club soda

Ice

Blueberry Lemonade

xxxxxx

The beautiful deep purple color makes this a hit with the kids.

Serves 6

Add blueberries, sugar, and 3 cups of water to a heavy saucepan. Bring to a boil over medium heat and simmer until the blueberries pop and the sugar is dissolved. Strain through a sieve to remove the pulp.

In a large pitcher, combine the lemon juice and water, then add the blueberry syrup. Add the superfine sugar and stir to dissolve. Pour into tall glasses over plenty of crushed ice. Garnish with blueberries and mint leaves.

3 cups blueberries

1 cup sugar

3 cups water

3 cups fresh lemon juice

5 cups cold water

1 cup superfine sugar

Crushed ice

Fresh blueberries, for garnish

Mint leaves, for garnish

Mom's Citrus Toddy

xxxxxx

Serves 4

2 1/2 **cups fresh grapefruit juice**

1 1/2 **cups fresh orange juice**

1/2 **cup honey**

1 **lemon, sliced**

4 **shots bourbon**

When you have a stuffy head and sore throat, there's nothing better than a little lemon and honey to make you feel better. You don't need to be sick to enjoy this yummy concoction on a cold winter night, and the best part is, there's plenty to share.

Heat the grapefruit and orange juices with the honey until the honey is melted and the mixture is hot. In each of 4 mugs, place several lemon slices and a shot of bourbon. Pour in the hot juice and stir.

Sangria Roja

xxxxxx

Serves 8

5 **lemons**

3 **oranges**

2 **cups water**

1 **cup sugar**

1/2 **cup brandy**

1/2 **cup Triple Sec**

1 **bottle (1 1/2 liters) dry red wine**

1 **quart club soda**

Crushed ice

As pretty as it is tasty, this makes a great summer party drink.

Slice the lemons and oranges into thin slices. Set aside the end pieces and wrap the rest in plastic. Refrigerate.

Place the end pieces in a saucepan with the water and sugar. Simmer over medium heat until the sugar is dissolved, about 5 minutes. Remove from heat and cool. Remove the fruit pieces and strain the resulting sugar syrup.

In a large pitcher or punch bowl, combine the sugar syrup, brandy, Triple Sec, and wine. Add sliced oranges and lemons, then pour in the club soda. Serve over crushed ice.

Pineapple Citrus Champagne Punch

xxxxxx

Champagne punch is a great celebration drink for bridal showers or other happy times.

Scrub the pineapples well, then peel and core them, removing the green tops. Set aside the flesh, and place the peels and cores in a large saucepan along with the lemon slices. Add the water and sugar. Bring to a boil over medium heat, then simmer for 30 minutes. Remove from heat and cool. Remove the fruit and strain the syrup, then chill.

In a large punch bowl, combine the chilled syrup with the orange and lemon juices. Chop the reserved pineapple, and add 1 cup of it to the punch bowl. Just before serving, add the Champagne. Float scoops of sorbet on top.

Serves 16

2 pineapples

3 lemons, thinly sliced

8 cups water

1 1/2 cups sugar

2 cups fresh orange juice, chilled

1/2 cup fresh lemon juice, chilled

2 bottles dry (brut) Champagne or sparkling wine, chilled

6 scoops orange sorbet

Sangria Blanca

xxxxxx

Serves 8

Use a crisp, yet inexpensive, Sauvignon Blanc to blend with the citrus flavors.

2 lemons

2 limes

2 oranges

2 cups water

1 cup sugar

1 bottle (1½ liters) dry white wine

¼ cup Triple Sec

Crushed ice

Slice the lemons, limes, and oranges, reserving the ends. Wrap the slices in plastic wrap and refrigerate.

Place the ends in a saucepan with the water and sugar. Bring to a boil over medium heat and cook until the sugar dissolves, about 5 minutes. Remove from heat and cool. Remove the fruit pieces and then strain.

In a large pitcher or punch bowl, combine the prepared syrup, white wine, and Triple Sec. Add the chilled fruit slices and ice.

The Perfect Margarita

xxxxxx

Jimmy Buffett may crave "that frozen concoction," but this is a much more refined version than what you'll find in a Parrot-head bar. Use the best tequila you can afford, serve on the rocks, and sip away to paradise.

Rub the lime wedge around the rim of the glass and then dip the rim in the salt. Add cracked ice to the glass.

Combine the tequila, Grand Marnier, and lime and orange juices in a cocktail shaker with a few ice cubes. Shake well, then pour into the salted glass filled with cracked ice. Squeeze the lime wedge into the glass.

Serves 1

1 lime wedge

1 tablespoon kosher salt

Cracked ice

1 ounce premium tequila plata (silver or white, sometimes called *blanco*)

1 ounce Grand Marnier

2 ounces fresh lime juice

2 ounces fresh orange juice

Ice cubes

Spicy Maria

XXXXXX

Serves 6

1 quart tomato juice

1/2 cup fresh lemon juice

2 tablespoons horseradish

1 teaspoon Rose's lime juice

1 teaspoon Worcestershire sauce

1/2 teaspoon hot pepper sauce

1 1/2 cups vodka

Cracked ice

Freshly ground black pepper

6 lime wedges

12 jalapeño-stuffed green olives

6 celery ribs, leafy tops intact

Specialty food stores usually carry a wide variety of hot sauces with differing levels of heat. Experiment until you find one that suits your taste. If you like it really spicy, use extra-hot horseradish.

Combine the tomato juice, lemon juice, horseradish, lime juice, Worcestershire sauce, and hot pepper sauce in a large pitcher, stirring well. Add the vodka and stir again. Pour into glasses filled with ice. Sprinkle each drink with black pepper to taste, then garnish with 1 lime wedge and 2 olives on a toothpick, along with one celery rib.